What's This TAIL Saying?

By Carolyn Combs ❀ Illustrated by Cathy Morrison

Dawn Publications

To Bobby and Niko with infinite gratitude for your love, support, and encouragement. Also to the scientists who spend countless hours observing animals so that we may better understand and protect them.—CC

To Talyn who loves all animals, from the tops of their heads to the tips of their very communicative tails.—CM

Library of Congress Cataloging-in-Publication Data

Names: Combs, Carolyn, 1969- author. | Morrison, Cathy, illustrator.
Title: What's this tail saying? / written by Carolyn Combs ; illustrated by Cathy Morrison.
Other titles: What is this tail saying?
Description: First edition. | Nevada City, CA : Dawn Publications, [2020] | Audience: Ages 3-8. | Audience: K to grade 3.
Identifiers: LCCN 2019013157| ISBN 9781584696612 (hardcover) | ISBN 9781584696629 (pbk.)
Subjects: LCSH: Animal communication--Juvenile literature. | Tail--Juvenile literature. | Body language--Juvenile literature.
Classification: LCC QL751.5 .C5945 2020 | DDC 591.59--dc23 LC record available at https://lccn.loc.gov/2019013157

Book design and computer production by
Patty Arnold, Menagerie Design and Publishing

Cover title font: Hopeless Heart
Interior fonts: Usherwood, Balzano, Formal 436, and Century Old Style
Illustrations: Digital painting

Manufactured by Regent Publishing Services, Hong Kong

Printed January 2020 in ShenZhen, Guangdong, China

10 9 8 7 6 5 4 3 2 1

First Edition

Dawn Publications
12402 Bitney Springs Road
Nevada City, CA 95959
www.dawnpub.com

Animal tails are talking. Can you guess what they are saying?

A fox kit inches too close.

Raise Wave

What's the skunk's tail saying?

Go away or I'll spray!

Oops! The kit learns a stinky lesson.

An egg thief is startled by a squawking mother bird.

Fluff Puff

What's the marmoset's tail saying?

I had a fright! Hold me tight!

The family cuddles and comforts the little one.

A wild horse doesn't see the rattlesnake coiled among the rocks.

Rattle Shake

What's the rattlesnake's tail saying?

Take flight or I'll bite!

Terrified, the horse skids to a stop
and then gallops away.

A coyote creeps toward the edge of the pond.

Wham Splash

What's the beaver's tail saying?

Stranger danger!

Hearing the alarm, the family dives into the pond.
They will be safe in deep water.

Two lion cubs wander away as they play.

Switch Twitch

What's the lioness's tail saying?

Don't stray. Follow this way.

The cubs notice their mother's tail
and scamper after her.

Big brother growls when a pup comes near.

Drop Tuck

What's the wolf pup's tail saying?

Don't be cross.
You're the boss!

The pup shows he doesn't want to fight,
and his brother leaves him alone.

While a peahen scratches for bugs, a peacock parades by.

Rustle Shiver

What's the peacock's tail saying?

Aren't I great?
Pick me as
your mate!

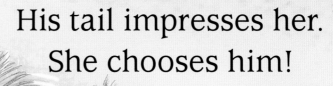

His tail impresses her.
She chooses him!

Uh-oh! A skink doesn't see the raccoon in time to run away.

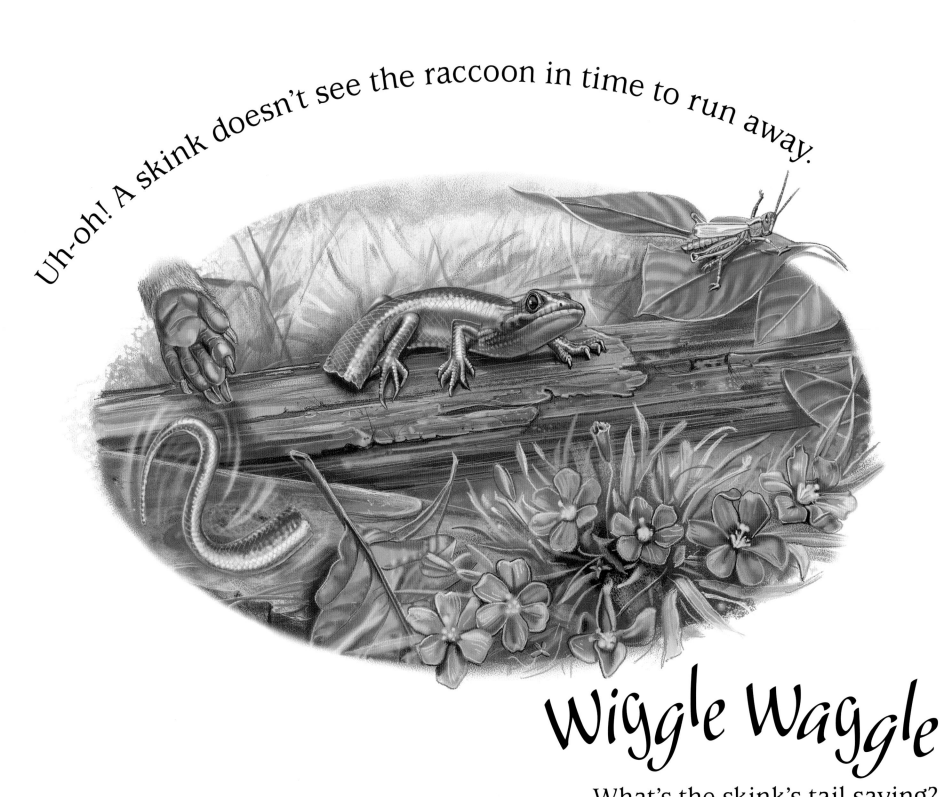

Wiggle Waggle

What's the skink's tail saying?

Come eat! I'll make a tasty treat!

The skink's escape trick works! The wiggling tail keeps the raccoon's attention while the skink hides.

From her perch, a little bird spots a hawk swooping in.

pump wag

What's the phoebe's tail saying?

You can't catch me!
So leave me be!

An alert phoebe is hard to catch.
The hawk flies off to find easier prey.

Elephant moms take a bath, but this calf isn't ready to join them.

Flip Zip

What's the calf's tail saying?

Race me! Chase me!

Sisters take turns running after each other.

A dolphin spies some tasty fish—enough for him and a few friends.

Smack Slap

What's the dolphin's tail saying?

Hey! Hey!
Follow me this way!

They fish together until their bellies are full.

Have any tails talked to you today?

More About Talking Tails

Spotted skunks often kick up into a handstand when they feel threatened. Then with the tail held high, they'll charge toward the enemy. The handstand makes the skunk look bigger and helps show off its coloring. Most animals know that the black-and-white spots warn of a stinky, blinding spray, and they choose to flee.

Coyotes, bears, bobcats, wolves, and eagles prey upon **North American beavers** as they gather mud and sticks on land. Using these materials, the beavers build dams. Deep pools of water form behind the dams. When predators approach, beavers dive into the pools. Their tails also act as rudders for swimming.

Common marmosets are hand-sized monkeys who scamper through the treetops of Brazil. Their ringed tails are longer than their bodies, but they can't hang from them. Only monkeys with grasping, prehensile tails can do that. Marmosets raise the hairs on their tails to show fear and ask for comfort.

In Africa, hungry leopards and hyenas hide in tall grasses, so **lionesses** keep their cubs close. The cubs can see their mother's tail above the grasses, even if they can't see her. Lions are the only members of the cat family with tasselled tails. The tassel makes a good fly swatter, too.

Snakes feel the ground moving when an animal approaches. **Western diamondback rattlesnakes** may rattle their tails as a warning, letting the other animal know where it is. If the animal turns away, the snake doesn't need to bite and saves its venom for its prey. New segments are added to the rattle as the snake grows and sheds its skin.

Gray wolves tuck their tails between their legs and crouch down to show they won't challenge stronger wolves. This message helps prevent fights and keeps younger and weaker wolves safe. A wolf will also wrap its tail around its body to stay warm when it lies down.

Male **Indian blue peafowl** rub their short tail feathers against their long, colorful train feathers. This makes the train vibrate. A big, bright vibrating train shows a male's good health and helps attract peahens. Peacocks shed their trains each year after mating season.

African elephants invite friends to play by moving their heads. Then, to show excitement and keep the play going, they raise their tails. Raised tails can also show fear. Traveling elephants form chains with tail-to-trunk links. This keeps the herd together and comforts calves.

Broad-headed skinks run away and hide from predators whenever possible. They only shed their tails for emergency escapes. Since they use their tails for balance and for storing fat, life is harder without their tails. It takes months for an adult to regrow its tail.

Atlantic bottlenose dolphins use tail splashes, called lobtails, to talk to other dolphins nearby. They also move themselves through the water by swishing their powerful tails up and down. Each lobe of a dolphin's tail is called a fluke.

Black phoebes pump their tails at predators like hawks. This signal tells the predator it's been spotted and won't easily catch the little bird. Predators need the element of surprise. They won't waste their energy swooping toward prey that will probably escape. Phoebe tails also help with steering, balancing, and braking.

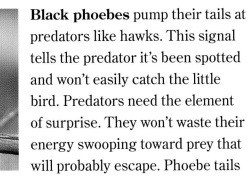

Dogs and cats communicate how they're feeling through their tails. A cat's tail held high usually means friendliness. A flicking or lashing tail may mean that the cat is agitated. A dog's wagging tail means that it is ready to interact. When the wagging is energetic and involves the hind end moving from side to side, too, it is a sign of joy or happiness.

A Word from the Author

Ever since I was a child, I've been captivated by how animals communicate. While researching this book, I not only learned about the way animals talk with their tails, but also about other ways they communicate. Their messages provide a window into the joys, struggles, and concerns they face. Glimpsing their inner worlds, even a little bit, enhances our ability to understand and appreciate animals on their own terms.

Literacy Connection: Tips for Reading Aloud

1. Before reading the book aloud, familiarize yourself with its two-page pattern—right pages show an illustration of an animal and a two-word sound or action that the animal's tail makes. A question at the bottom of the page asks, "What's this [animal's] tail saying?" Left pages reveal the answer through a rhyming verse, followed by a short explanation about what happened as a result of the communication. There are two exceptions to this pattern—a peacock and a skink cover three pages each.

2. As you read the book aloud, emphasize the sounds and movements of each tail. Pause after asking the question and have children look closely at the illustration for clues before taking their responses. Then turn the page and read the answer and the result of the communication.

3. Read aloud and discuss the information on the "Explore More for Kids" pages. Follow up by doing one or more of the suggested activities.

Social Emotional Learning: Communication Skills

Learning about animal communication provides a natural springboard to introduce human communication. The Collaborative for Academic, Social, and Emotional Learning (CASEL) provides the following information for developing relationship skills through effective communication:

🍃 **Communicate clearly:** Communication involves not only speaking clearly and conveying ideas appropriately, but also understanding body language, facial expressions, and gestures that can contribute to accurate delivery and perception.

🍃 **Listen well:** Active listening depends on the ability to consciously make the effort to hear and comprehend what the other person is saying and respond appropriately. Some foundational skills involved in active listening include appropriate eye contact, regulating thoughts to limit distractions, utilizing facial expressions, and providing oral responses.

In the book, animals use their tails to send a message (nonverbal communication). What animal did not receive the message that was being sent? (fox kit) Practice nonverbal communication by acting out simple messages and having the class guess what you're saying through your body movements and facial expression. You may begin with simple classroom directions such as "Place your paper here," "Line up to go outside," and "It's time for reading." You may also act out feelings such as happiness, sadness, fear, relief, or disappointment. Invite children to act out messages for the class to guess.

STEAM Activities

SCIENCE — Using Scientific Practices

Scientists often begin their research by using their senses to make **observations**. Then scientists make guesses about what the observations mean. These guesses are called **hypotheses** (singular: hypothesis). Explain to children that they were making observations when they looked carefully for clues in the illustrations and that their guesses about what the animals' tails were saying were hypotheses.

Invite children to keep practicing being scientists by watching their pets or other animals. After carefully looking and listening, they can make guesses about what animals are saying with their tails or other body parts. They can ask an expert or look in a book to see if their guesses are correct.

TECHNOLOGY — Putting on Your Animal Ears

Review the sounds that some tails make by asking *What sound does a beaver's tail make?* (wham splash) *Peacock's tail?* (rustle shiver) *Dolphin's tail?* (smack slap) *Rattlesnake's tail?* (rattle shake). Play a youtube video so children can listen to the sound of a rattlesnake shaking its tail.

🍃 Rattlesnake sound: https://www.youtube.com/watch?v=vaSeSIZ9Fgw.

Demonstrate how to listen with "animal ears" by cupping your hands behind your ears in a forward-facing C-shape. Have children put on their animal ears and replay the rattlesnake audio. Ask *What difference did you notice in the sounds?* Repeat the process listening to the rustle of a peacock's tail, first without animal ears and then with them. Conclude by taking students for a walk and have them use their animal ears to listen to the sounds around them.

🍃 Peacock sound: https://www.youtube.com/watch?v=OFg7CPI0f20.

ENGINEERING — Creating Tails, Part One

Invite children to create a tail for an animal (either real or imaginary). Have students complete a "Design Sheet," which may include a sketch of the animal, its name, a brief description of the tail, and the message their tail will communicate.

ART — Creating Tails, Part Two

Using the information from their "Design Sheet," have students create a model of their tail. Provide them with a variety of craft supplies, including some items that make noise such as beads, beans, or seeds. When finished, have students demonstrate their tails (they may wear them) and invite the class to guess what the tail is saying. Discuss the design features of each tail and ask the students *What worked in your design? What didn't work? What would you do differently next time?*

MATH — Longer or Shorter

The tails of the animals presented in the book vary in size from 3 to 52 inches (7 to 142 cm). Download directions for a hands on math activity that compares tail sizes at www.dawnpub.com/activity. Scroll down and click on *What's This Tail Saying?* A student handout of tail sizes is also available, along with additional activities and standards-based lesson plans.

Carolyn Combs is a former molecular biologist who now shares her passion for the natural world with children through her writing. She still loves doing research, but now does it at the library, online, and by speaking with scientists rather than researching in a lab. She has fond memories from her childhood of camping beside a noisy beaver dam and of visiting a local petting farm and waiting for the peacock to fan out his tail. These memories, along with her curiosity about animal communication, helped inspire her to write this book—her first picture book. Carolyn lives in Michigan with her husband, son, poodle, cat, and guinea pig, who runs around her feet and oinks while she writes. Find her at carolyncombsbooks.com.

Cathy Morrison is an award-winning illustrator who lives in Northern Colorado, within view of both the Great Plains and the Rocky Mountains. She began her career in animation and graphic design, but she discovered her passion for children's book illustration while raising her two children.

After several years illustrating with traditional media, she now works digitally. Cathy loves researching the animals she draws, but she came a little too close for comfort when she walked right up to one outside her home. It really did go *Rattle Shake*! This is Cathy's seventh book for Dawn Publications. Visit her "Studio With A View" blog at www.cathymorrison.blogspot.com.

If you draw it, they will come.

More Nature Books from Dawn Publications

Tall Tall Tree—Take a peek at some of the animals that make their home in a magnificent redwood. Rhyming verses and a 1-10 counting scheme make this a real page-turner.

Why Should I Walk? I Can Fly!—A little bird, a big sky, and the first time out of the nest. A robin's first flight is a gentle reminder about what we can accomplish if we just keep trying.

Silent Swoop: An Owl, an Egg, and a Warm Shirt Pocket—A true story of the relationship between a Great Horned Owl and the person who rescued him.

Scampers Thinks Like a Scientist—Scampers is no ordinary mouse! Her infectiously experimental spirit will have young readers eager to think like scientists too.

Over on the Desert: Somewhere in the World—Are deserts empty? Nope! They're filled with life, color, and lots of action!

Also Illustrated by Cathy Morrison

Baby on Board: How Animals Carry Their Young—Discover many clever ways animals carry their babies.

The Prairie That Nature Built—Go above, below, and all around this beautiful and exciting habitat.

Pitter and Patter—Take a ride with Pitter and Patter, two water drops, as they flow through the water cycle.

If You Love Honey: Nature's Connections—Honey is a sweet gift from nature—ALL of nature!

Over on the Farm—Welcome to the farm, where pigs roll, goats nibble, horses gallop, hens peck, and turkeys strut!

Wild Ones: Observing City Critters—Animals are everywhere in the city! Look closely to meet them.

Dawn Publications is dedicated to inspiring in children a deeper understanding and appreciation for all life on Earth. You can browse through our titles, download resources for teachers, and order at www.dawnpub.com or call 800-545-7475.